A GIFT FOR:

Phyllis

FROM:

Jim, Valerie, Cullen and Cole

Dec. 25, 2013

God has brought me laughter.

Genesis 21:6

AN *INHERIT THE MIRTH* CARTOON COLLECTION BY CUYLER BLACK

WHAT'S THAT FUNNY LOOK ON YOUR FAITH?

gift books

Sometimes even God gets junk mail.
TIRED OF MOVING IN MYSTERIOUS WAYS??
CALL AL'S VAN LINES
1-800-555-2337

MUSIC MINISTRIES OF THE ANIMAL KINGDOM.
Okay, I admit it. A handbell choir was a bad idea.

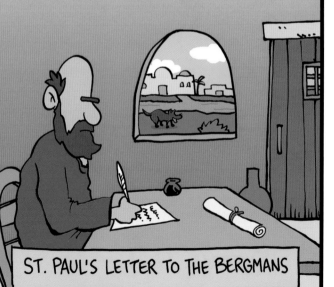

You're naming me "Eve"? Good! That's better than what he came up with!
RIB-ECCA
RIB-ERTA

Could you leave the bubble wrap alone for five seconds and look at these?!
pop! pop pop! pop poppity pop! Pop! Pop! pop! poppity pop! pop pop! pop
TEN COMMAND-MENTS
FRAGILE

YOUTH GROUP FUNDRAISERS IN BIBLICAL TIMES.

AFTER 40 DAYS AND NIGHTS ON THE ARK, NOAH'S MISSION FOR GOD IS COMPLETED.
Is it true? God sent us a thank-you gift?
2-WEEK OCEAN CRUISE

THE GREAT HYMNS
Amazing grace,
how sweet the sound,
that saved a wretch
like my brother despite the fact
he never helps with the dishes.
Ever.
FIRST DRAFT.

These are the ones He wants us to stay away from.
TREE of the KNOWLEDGE of GOOD and EVIL
TREE of the KNOWLEDGE of HOW to CREATE POLKA MUSIC

REV. BARNES HEADS OFF ON ANOTHER PASTORAL CALL.

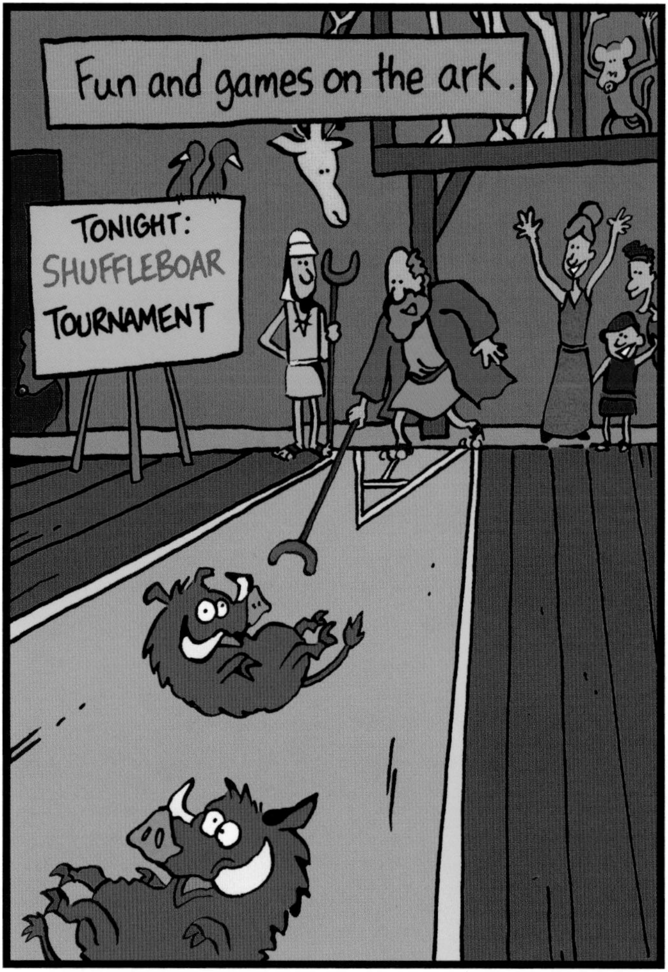
Fun and games on the ark.
TONIGHT:
SHUFFLEBOAR
TOURNAMENT

SILENT NIGHT. HOLY NIGHT. AL IS CALM. AL IS BRIGHT.
Relax, friends. Stand on a sheep and you'll see just fine.
Good thinking, Al!

ANCIENT PEOPLES OF THE OLD TESTAMENT.

THE ISRAELITES

THE MIDIANITES

THE AMMONITES

THE OVERBITES

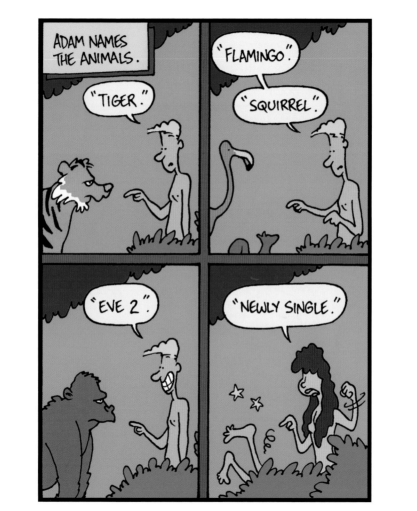

IT TOOK SOME TIME FOR MOSES TO DECIDE WHAT TO CALL THE FIRST BOOK OF THE BIBLE.
God Gets Busy
It's Showtime!
Ready or Not, Here Comes the Universe
Existence! Gotta Love It!
Genesis

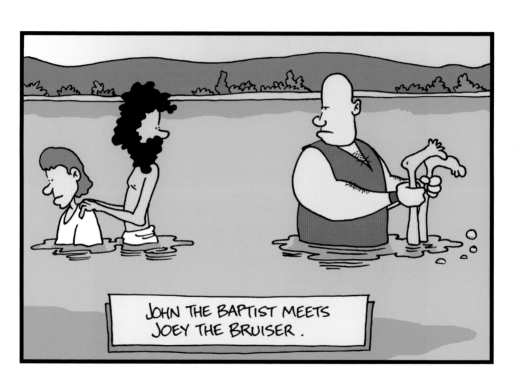

JOHN THE BAPTIST MEETS
JOEY THE BRUISER.

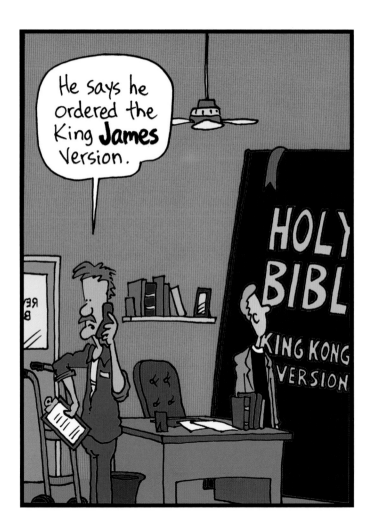

VALENTINE'S DAY IN THE GARDEN OF EDEN.
Y'Know, this might have been more of a head-scratcher if we weren't the only two people on the planet.
To EVE, from A SEcrEt AdmiRER

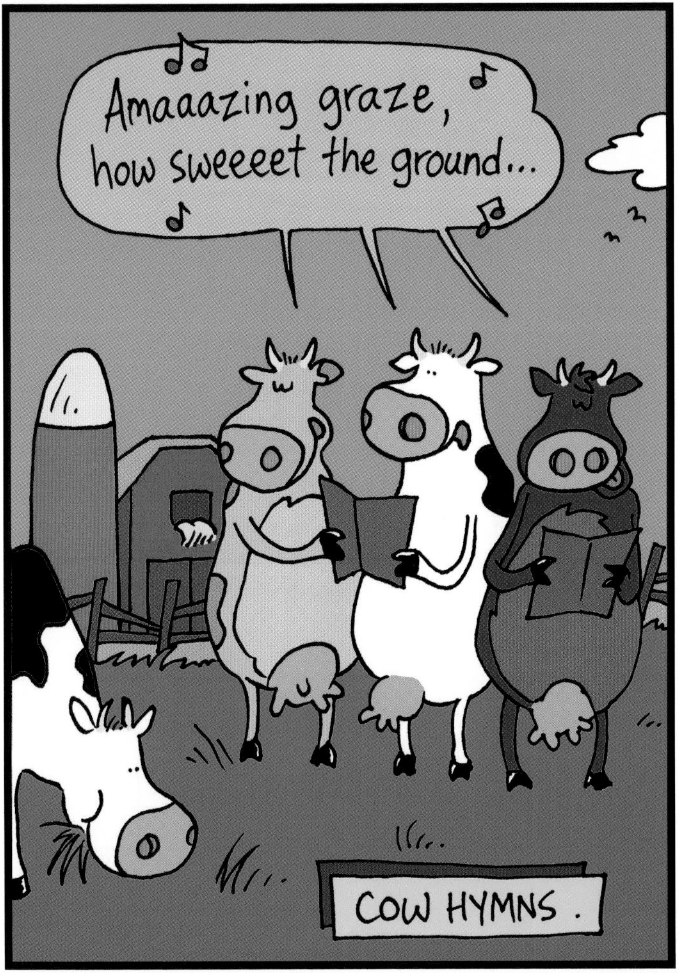
Amaaazing graze, how sweeeet the ground...
COW HYMNS.

Hey, Jesus, that was amazing how you turned the water into wine over there! Could you change these sticks into a set of bath towels? I forgot to bring a wedding gift.

Honey, for the last time—
stop doing that to the pets!
JOHN THE BAPTIST AS A KID.

Every time we tell him the play's been whistled "dead," he says "No big deal" and keeps going!
Why the disciples didn't like playing football with Lazarus

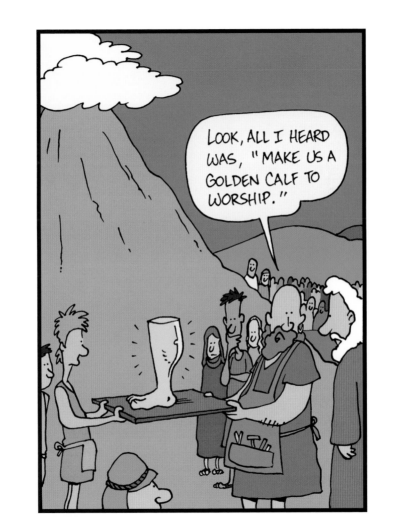

GOD WELCOMES ADAM AND EVE TO THE GARDEN OF EDEN.
Very funny.
NO SHIRT, NO SHOES, NO SERVICE

ADAM AND EVE AND THEIR TEENAGE DAUGHTER.
It's called a BELLY BUTTON RING! You don't HAVE belly buttons, so you don't understand!

If you have enjoyed this book
or it has touched your life in some way,
we would love to hear from you.

Please send your comments to:
Hallmark Book Feedback
P.O. Box 419034
Mail Drop 215
Kansas City, MO 64141

Or e-mail us at:
booknotes@hallmark.com